Design by Jennifer Tramel
Photography by Renae Johnson
Editing by Shajan Clay

I'm Happy Being GLUTEN Free

a kid's COOKBOOK

from a kid's point of view

WRITTEN BY SIERRA METZGER
PHOTOGRAPHED BY RENEE JOHNSON
DESIGNED BY JENNIFER TRAMEL

INTRODUCTION

Gluten is a natural protein found in foods such as wheat, rye, and barley. It is found in most types of cereal and in many types of bread. However, there are some grains that don't contain gluten. Some grains that don't contain gluten are wild rice, corn, buckwheat, soybeans and sunflower seeds.

A gluten-free diet means avoiding all foods made from or containing wheat, rye, barley and usually, oats.

I always read the label of all food items. I look for words that say gluten-free. Sometimes labels say wheat free but these foods may contain oats.

I also look for the allergy warning. Some food labels say:
- "May contain wheat."
- "Produced in a plant that also produces products made with wheat."
- "Produced on equipment that also produces products that contain wheat."

There are certain ingredients you have to look for:

Hydrolyzed Corn, Soy, or Vegetable Protein

> All of these can possibly contain gluten. Wheat is often used in the process of making these proteins (because gluten is a protein). Of these, hydrolyzed vegetable protein is most likely to have gluten in it.

Soy Sauce

> Soy sauce is made with wheat.

Malt

> Malt is sometimes also called barley malt. All malt is made from barley, even if it is called "rice malt."

(Modified) Food Starch

> Not all food starch contains gluten but, unless you know what kind of starch it is (i.e. corn starch or wheat starch) it is best to avoid it..

Some foods with gluten (breads, pastas, and pastries) are easy to spot. Others can be harder to identify. Here are a few to look out for:

Dairy

> Sometimes starch fillers are added to yogurt and soft cheeses.

Cereal

> Most cereal contain some form of gluten. For example, cornflakes contain malt.

Canned Soups, Stews, and Frozen Meals

> Look for starch fillers, soy sauce, hydrolyzed vegetable protein and pasta.

TABLE of CONTENTS

Breakfast

Lunch

Dinner

Soup, Salad & Such

Dessert

Just for Fun

Snacks & Other Stuff

\ˈbrek-fəst \

noun

The first meal
of the day,
usually eaten in
the morning.

Chocolate Chip Pancakes

Ingredients:

- 1 cup gluten-free pancake mix
- 2/3 cups milk
- 1 egg
- 1 teaspoon oil
- 1/2 cup chocolate chip morsels
- syrup (as much as you desire)

TIP

When you see lots of bubbles form on top of the pancake that means it's time to flip.

Directions:

1. In a large bowl, combine pancake mix, milk, egg, oil, and chocolate chip morsels and mix.
2. Preheat large non-stick skillet over medium heat until hot and add non-stick cooking spray. Hold your hand 2 inches above skillet. If you feel the heat, it's ready. DO NOT TOUCH!
3. Pour pancake mixture slowly onto center of the skillet until you form a big circle.
4. Let the pancake brown on one side then flip to the other side until golden brown.
5. Repeat steps 3 and 4 with remaining mixture.
6. Serve with syrup... Enjoy!

French Toast & Berries

Ingredients:

- 2 slices gluten-free bread
- 2 eggs
- 1/2 cup milk
- 1 teaspoon cinnamon
- 1 teaspoon gluten-free vanilla extract
- Non-stick cooking spray or 2 tablespoons butter
- 1/3 cup blueberries (optional)
- 1 teaspoon powdered sugar (optional)
- syrup (as much as desired)

Directions:

1. Combine eggs, milk, cinnamon, and vanilla in a medium bowl and stir.
2. Preheat large non-stick skillet and add non-stick cooking spray or butter.
3. Take 1 slice of bread and soak in egg mixture on first side for 5 seconds. Flip to the other side and soak for in mixture for about 5 seconds.
4. Transfer bread to skillet, cook on each side flipping with a spatula until golden brown.
5. Repeat steps 3 and 4 on the second slice of bread.
6. Remove from skillet and top with blueberries (if desired).
7. Dust lightly with powdered sugar (if desired) and serve with syrup.

Scrambled Eggs & Cheese

Ingredients:

- 3 eggs
- 1 dash salt
- 1 pinch black pepper
- 1/4 cup shredded cheese
- 2 teaspoons olive oil

Mmm Good!

I find that a hard rubber spatula works best when scrambling eggs.

Directions:

1. In a large bowl, add eggs, salt, and pepper. Whip together using a whisk.
2. Set mixture aside, preheat large skillet, and add olive oil, (to see if the skillet is hot enough, hold your hand about 2 inches above it to feel for the heat).
3. Pour egg mixture into the heated skillet and let cook. Add cheese once the egg begins to bubble.
4. Using a spatula, break eggs up and turn them over and over until eggs are no longer running.
5. Remove from skillet and serve alone or with your favorite breakfast meat.

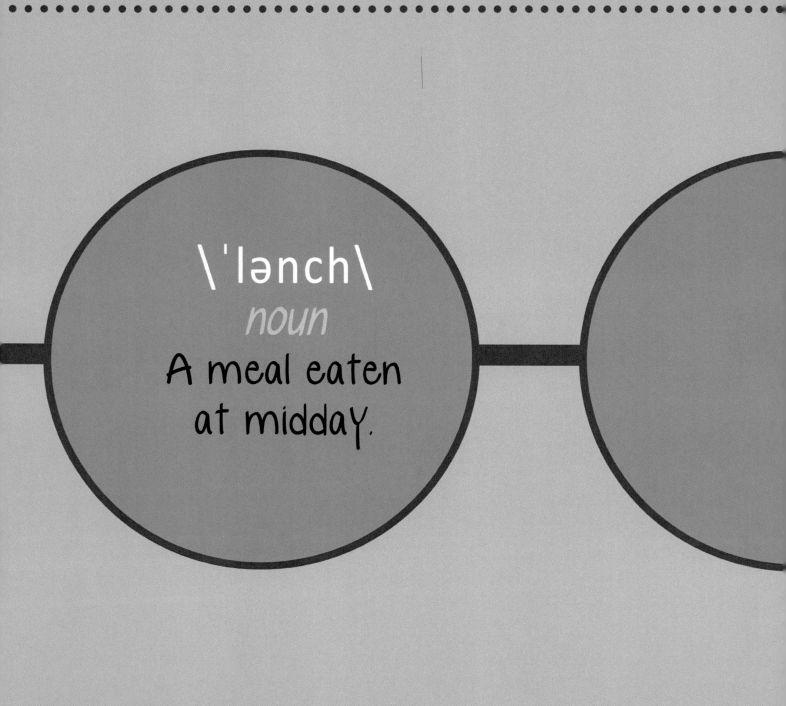

Chili Dog Panini

Ingredients:

- 1 tablespoon gluten-free chili
- 1 hot dog cut in half horizontally (from tip to tip)
- 2 slices gluten-free sandwich bread
- 2 slices of cheese
- Non-stick cooking spray

Directions:

1. Cook split hot dog in microwave for 1 minute
2. Spray non-stick cooking spray on both sides of the Panini maker.
3. Layer 1st slice of bread on the Panini maker.
4. Add 1st slice of cheese.
5. Place both halves of the hotdog on top of cheese.
6. Add 1 tablespoon of chili in the center of the hotdogs.
7. Add 2nd slice of cheese on top of the hotdogs and chili.
8. Add 2nd slice of bread on top of the hotdogs, chili, and cheese.
9. Close and lock Panini maker and let cook for 7 minutes.

Did You Know?

In **Italy**, a Panini is simply a sandwich, but in other parts of the world, people call them grilled Panini, a hot sandwich made by pressing the sandwich in a grill for a few minutes before serving.

Pepperoni & Cheese Quesadilla

Ingredients:

- Gluten-free Turkey Pepperoni
- 1 cup shredded mozzarella cheese
- 2 corn tortillas
- Non-stick cooking spray
- 1 tablespoon gluten-free pizza sauce

Mmm Good!

Corn tortillias are **great** to make any type of gluten-free sandwich!

Directions:

1. Spray a skillet with non-stick cooking spray.
2. Preheat skillet on medium heat.
3. Lay 1st corn tortilla in skillet.
4. Add 1 teaspoon of pizza sauce to the center of tortilla.
5. Layer 1/2 cup of mozzarella cheese on corn tortilla.
6. Place pepperoni on top of cheese (space it out where you can still see cheese underneath).
7. Layer remainder of mozzarella cheese on top of pepperoni.
8. Add remainder of pizza sauce on the top of mozzarella cheese.
9. Place the 2nd corn tortilla on top of pepperoni.
10. Use spatula to flatten Quesadilla and heat until golden brown on one side.
11. Flip and brown opposite side until golden brown.

HOT DOG!
It's a Rolly Cheese Polly

Ingredients:

- 2 beef or chicken gluten-free hot dogs
- 2 slices pepper jack cheese
- 2 corn tortillas
- 2 wooden toothpicks
- 2 tablespoons of ketchup (optional)

Directions:

1. Preheat oven to 350 degrees.
2. Lay corn tortilla flat on counter.
3. Layer cheese in the center of the corn tortilla.
4. Lay hot dog on the edge of corn tortilla and roll slowly.
5. After rolling neatly, stick a toothpick in the center of the corn tortilla to hold ingredients together.
6. Place each roll side-by-side in a baking dish.
7. Bake for 15 minutes.
8. Remove from oven and let cool for 5 minutes.
9. Serve with ketchup. (optional)

23

\ˈdi-nər\

noun

The chief meal of the day, eaten in the evening or at midday.

DINNER

Spaghetti

Ingredients:

- 4 ounce box of gluten-free spaghetti pasta
- 1 jar red tomato and basil sauce
- 1 small tomato, diced
- 1 teaspoon fresh garlic, *minced**
- 1 pound ground turkey
- 1 tablespoon olive oil
- 2 teaspoons seasoning salt

*Mince

To cut or chop into very small pieces.

Directions:

1. Cook pasta according to directions on box, and set aside.
2. Add oil to a skillet and preheat over medium-low heat.
3. Add turkey and seasoning salt to skillet,. Cook turkey continuously stirring to prevent clumps.
4. In a medium-sized pot on medium heat, add tomato sauce and diced tomatoes.
5. Add browned ground turkey to sauce and diced tomatoes.
6. Cook for 15 minutes on medium heat.
7. Place pasta on a plate and top with spaghetti sauce.

28

Mac & Cheese

Ingredients:

- Gluten-free rice shells
- 1 pack of shredded cheddar cheese
- 1/2 stick butter
- 1 cup half & half or milk
- 4 ounces of cream cheese

Directions:

1. Preheat oven to 350 degrees.
2. Cook rice shells according to directions on box.
3. Preheat medium saucepan on low heat. Add butter, milk, cream cheese and 1/2 pack of shredded cheese to pan and heat until smooth. Remove pan from oven.
4. In a baking dish, add pasta and cheese sauce.
5. Sprinkle remainder of shredded cheese on top.
6. Place mac & cheese in oven and bake for 25 minutes or until top is golden brown.

Vita-good!

Milk and cheese have an important nutrient called calcium that helps bones grow strong!

Turkey & Cheese Pizza

Ingredients:

- Gluten-free pizza crust
- 1/2 cup cooked ground turkey
- 1 cup Kraft Cheese
- 1/4 cup mushrooms
- 1/2 cup gluten-free pizza sauce
- Non-stick cooking spray

Directions:

1. Preheat oven to 350 degrees.
2. Spray cooking spray on a baking sheet.
3. Place pizza crust in the center of baking sheet.
4. Take a large spoon and scoop pizza sauce onto the crust. Use the back of the spoon to spread the sauce evenly on crust.
5. Add cooked ground turkey evenly over sauce.
6. Layer mushrooms evenly on top of pizza.
7. Top evenly with cheese.
8. Bake for 20 minutes.
9. Remove from oven and let cool for 10 minutes.
10. Use pizza cutter to cut pizza into square or triangle slices, whichever you prefer.

\\'süp\

noun

A liquid food prepared from meat, fish, or vegetable stock combined with various other ingredients and often containing solid pieces.

\\'sa-ləd\

noun

A dish of raw leafy green vegetables, often tossed with pieces of other vegetables, fruit, cheese, or other ingredients and served with a dressing.

Chicken Noodle Soup

Ingredients:

- 1 cup cooked, chopped chicken (great use of mom's leftovers)
- 1 cup diced carrots
- 1/2 cup diced celery
- 1 24 ounce can chicken broth
- 1/2 box gluten-free spaghetti noodles

*Simmer

Simmer means to cook gently or remain just at or below the boiling point.

Directions:

1. In a medium sized pot, bring chicken broth to a low boil.
2. Add carrots and celery. Cook until tender.
3. Stir in chicken and *simmer.
4. In a separate pot, cook spaghetti according to directions on box.
5. Drain spaghetti, add to soup, and stir.
6. Remove from heat, let cool, and serve.

Croutons & Salad

Ingredients:

- 3 slices gluten-free sandwich bread
- 1 teaspoon onion powder
- 2 tablespoons olive oil
- 3 small romaine lettuce leaves

- 3/4 cherry tomatoes
- 1 teaspoon garlic powder
- 2 slices tomatoes cut into cubes
- 1/4 cup shredded carrots
- 2 tablespoons gluten-free dressing

Directions for Croutons:

1. Preheat oven to 350 degrees.
2. Cut edges off bread and cut into cubes.
3. Place bread in large bowl.
4. Mix olive oil, garlic powder and onion powder in a small bowl.
5. Pour oil seasoning mixture onto bread and stir, making sure bread is thoroughly covered.
6. Lay parchment paper on baking sheet and spread all the bread cubes flat on sheet.
7. Bake for 45 minutes or until bread cubes are dry and golden brown.
8. Remove from oven and cool.

Directions for Salad:

1. Tear romaine lettuce into small pieces and place in a large bowl.
2. Dice tomatoes into small pieces and add to lettuce.
3. Add carrots to salad.
4. Top with croutons and serve.

For extra crunchy croutons after baking, turn oven off oven and leave croutons in the oven for about 20 minutes.

Mixed Berry Smoothie

Ingredients:

- 1/2 cup frozen strawberries
- 1/4 cup frozen blueberries
- 1 whole banana cut into small pieces
- 1 cup Welch's White Grape Juice
- 1 cup chopped ice

Directions:

1. Put all the ingredients in a blender and blend until texture is smooth and all the ice is completely blended.
2. Serve in your favorite cup.

39

\di-ˈzərt\
noun

A usually sweet course
or dish, as of fruit, ice
cream, or pastry,
served at the
end of a meal.

White Chocolate Rice Krispie Treats

Ingredients:

- 3 tablespoons butter or margarine
- 4 cups miniature marshmallows
- 6 cups gluten-free brown rice krispies
- 1 teaspoon vanilla extract
- 1 cup white chocolate morsels
- 1/2 cup macadamia nut pieces

Remember!

Some cereal made with rice flour can also contain gluten if it contains malt or malt flavoring. Check the label!

Directions:

1. Grease a 13 x 9 inch baking pan.
2. In a large non-stick skillet, melt butter over low heat.
3. Add marshmallows to skillet and stir until completely melted.
4. Remove marshmallows from heat.
5. Add vanilla extract to marshmallows.
6. Gently stir in rice krispies, chocolate morsels, and macadamia nuts.
7. Pour mixture onto greased baking pan.
8. Apply butter to spatula so it doesn't stick to your mixture. Use buttered spatula to press mixture flat.
9. Cut into squares and serve.

*A ramekin is a single-serving dish that is used to prepare and serve food in.

Quick Caramel Apple Pie

Ingredients:

- 4 Ramekins*
- 2 apples
- 2 tablespoon sugar
- 1 teaspoon cinnamon

- 3 tablespoons butter
- 2 cups gluten-free ginger snaps
- Caramel with squeeze top
- 1 gallon size plastic Ziploc Bag
- Rolling pin

Directions:

1. Preheat oven to 350 degrees.
2. Place ginger snaps in Ziploc bag and seal.
3. Take the rolling pin and roll over bag until ginger snaps are crumbled into large and small pieces.
4. Add a pat of butter to each Ramekin.
5. Peel and dice one red apple (you may need an adult's assistance...I'm still learning to peel apples, but with a lot of practice, I'm getting better at it).
6. Preheat skillet on low heat and add butter.
7. After melting butter in skillet, add apples, cinnamon, and sugar.
8. Continuously stir apple mixture until apples are soft and tender. Remove from heat.
9. Take the larger pieces of crumbled ginger snaps from the Ziploc and place them in the Ramekins on top of butter.
10. Put apple mixture on top of large cookie crumbles.
11. Pour smaller cookie crumbles on top of apples.
12. Drizzle caramel on top creating a large "Z" or 5 dots.
13. Place Ramekins on a baking sheet.
14. Bake on 350 degrees for 20 minutes or until brown.
15. Remove from oven and let Ramekins cool for 10 minutes before serving.

Cheesecake

Ingredients:

- 1 bag gluten-free gingersnaps
- 5 tablespoons butter
- 1 tablespoon brown sugar
- 1 box unflavored gelatin
- 1 tablespoon vanilla
- 1/2 cup sugar
- 2 teaspoons freshly squeezed lemon juice
- 1 pie pan
- 2 8 ounce packs cream cheese (room temperature)

Directions:

1. In a food processor, blend ginger snaps until the texture is smooth with no chunks (a blender can be used as well).
2. Mix gingersnap crumbs, butter, and brown sugar in a bowl. Stir until mixture is well blended (color should be a dark brown throughout).
3. Pour ginger snap mixture into a pie pan and spread evenly using a large spoon, press flat in pie pan and set aside.
4. Combine gelatin and sugar in a bowl, mix well.
5. Add cream cheese to gelatin mixture and use a food blender to mix thoroughly.
6. Slowly add lemon juice.
7. Pick up bowl and use a small icing spatula to assist in pouring mixture evenly on top of gingersnap crust. Use spatula to spread cream cheese evenly (spread gently so that ginger-snap crust stays in place).
8. Cool for 2 hours.
9. Use a knife and cut into triangle slices.

\\ˈfən\\

noun

A source of enjoyment, amusement, or pleasure.

Caramel Balls

Ingredients:

- 1 3 1/2 ounce bag plain microwave popcorn
- 1 cup brown sugar
- 1 stick butter
- 1/2 cup corn syrup
- 1/4 teaspoon salt

Directions:

1. Pop popcorn, place in a medium bowl, and set aside.
2. In a medium saucepan, combine brown sugar, 5 tablespoons butter, corn syrup, and salt.
3. Heat over medium heat stirring constantly for 5 minutes until mixture is smooth.
4. Remove from heat, pour over popcorn, and stir well. [WARNING: Mixture will be very hot. Allow to cool for 5 minutes, but be careful not to let it get cold.]
5. While mixture is warm, cover your hands with butter and quickly shape mixture into balls.
6. Place caramel balls on a platter and serve.

Yogurt Parfait

Ingredients:

- 8 ounce gluten-free vanilla yogurt
- 1/4 cup gluten-free, rice cereal crumbled (use hands to break up)
- 1/4 cup fresh blueberries
- 1/4 cup of fresh strawberries, sliced

Directions:

1. Spoon 1/4 cup of yogurt into a parfait glass.
2. Add a layer of blueberries and strawberries.
3. Repeat steps 1 and 2.
4. Finally, top with crumbled cereal.

Movie Mix

MOVIE MIX

Ingredients:

- 3 cups rice gluten-free cereal
- 1 mini-bag of microwave popcorn with butter
- 2 boxes of yogurt covered raisins
- 4 ounce unsalted mixed-nuts (optional)

Directions:

1. Mix all ingredients in a large bowl. Enjoy!

\\'snak\\

noun

A small quantity of food; light meal or refreshment taken between regular meals.

SNACKS & OTHER STUFF

Around the house...

At first, finding gluten-free snacks was a challenge. But, when I figured out that a lot of the snacks I enjoyed before I became gluten-free were good for me, it wasn't hard at all. Just look around your kitchen...you will be surprised at all the delicious gluten-free snacks you can enjoy!

- Sliced apples and peanut butter
- Celery and peanut butter
- Cucumbers and gluten-free ranch dressing
- Corn chips and salsa
- Make a lettuce roll with lettuce, turkey slice and cheese slice
- Frozen grapes
- Gluten-free cereal in a snack bag
- Hard-boiled egg and a sprinkle of salt & pepper
- Orange slices
- Sliced tomato and a sprinkle of salt & pepper
- 1 toasted gluten-free waffle
- Juice in a small plastic cup and freeze (eat with a spoon)
- Toast a slice of gluten-free bread and spread your favorite gluten-free jelly
- Cheese and rice crackers
- Add mayonnaise to a can of tuna and sprinkle with salt & pepper

Remember...

Whenever mom or dad brings something new home from the grocery store, READ THE LABEL! Even if it's food you eat all the time. Companies sometime change their ingredients. Don't just assume the ingredients are the same. WE ARE RESPONSIBLE FOR OUR OWN BODIES!

How to recognize gluten allergies...

Some people have extreme allergies to gluten. When they are exposed to gluten they become ill. It could take weeks to recover and some may even be hospitalized. People with extreme gluten allergies have to avoid foods that have cross contamination. Cross contamination is when food is gluten-free but may have been prepared with utensils used to prepare food that contains gluten. Or, food is gluten-free but may have been prepared on the same lines the manufacturer uses to prepare food that contains gluten..

Fortunately, I simply have a gluten allergy and my side affects from gluten are only temporary. Cross contamination is important to my family but not as severe as someone with Celiacs Disease.

Here is a list of symptoms of a gluten allergy:

- Gas troubles
- Diarrhea or constipation
- Gastric reflux or heartburn
- Tired
- Uncomfortable tummy
- Lack of energy
- Not growing well
- Eczema

- Runny nose and sinus problems
- Feel depressed and/or moody
- Find it hard to think clearly
- Headaches or migraines
- Trouble Sleeping
- Attention Deficit Hyperactivity Disorder (ADHD)
- Hyperactivity

Snacks on the move...

Iknow you are familiar with hanging out to long on a Saturday with your mom at the mall, or you're at the convience stand with a friend at a game, or you're at a movie and forgot to pack snacks. What do you eat? There are a few familiar brands you might find that are gluten-free and safe to eat. Remember no matter how many times you've purchased this item, take the time before you purchase to read the label. Even if the customers behind you seem impatient and are screaming "HURRY UP!" Take your time and read the label, this is your health and that customer doesn't understand how one wrong ingredient can ruin a great night.

- **Lays Stax Chips**
  all flavors are gluten-free
- **Planters Nuts**
  gluten-free
- **Welche's Fruit Snacks**
  gluten-free
- **Tostidos***
- **Cheetos***
- **Lays Original Potato Chips***
- **Snickers Candy Bars***

*Cross Contamination

Indicates that products are gluten-free but are produced on the same lines as products that contain gluten. Although the lines are washed between batches, a slight residue may remain on the lines. This is called **cross contamination**. Individuals who are extremely sensitive to gluten may be affected.

Birthday parties...

If you get that invite for a birthday party, you have to pack your snacks in advance. I usually pack gluten-free cookies or a brownie. If ice cream is served at the party, feel free to enjoy your gluten-free dessert along with the ice cream. Some ice cream, depending on the flavor and brand, is not gluten-free. It's a good idea to have your mom call the adult in charge of the party in advance to ask about the menu and inform them of your allergy. Some gluten-free kids fear drawing attention to themselves because of their special diet. A conversation your parent might have could go something like this.

Birthday Kid's Mom: "I was planning on serving Breyer's Vanilla ice cream."

My Mom: "Great! Breyer's Vanilla Ice Cream is gluten-free. If you don't mind, Sierra will bring a gluten-free snack to go along with the ice cream since she can't eat cake. Thank you for your patience and the invite to the party. We will see you on Saturday!"

Or if you choose, you can take your own gluten-free ice cream along with your gluten-free dessert and have your parent ask if you can store your ice cream in the freezer until it's time to eat cake and ice cream.

Foods that contain gluten...

The following items are usually sources of gluten (the exception would be a specially-made gluten-free versions):

- Bagels
- Biscuits
- Bread
- Bread Crumbs
- Breaded Fish
- Breaded Meats
- Breaded Poultry
- Bread Pudding
- Cake
- Cereal
- Chicken Nuggets
- Croissants
- Cookies
- Doughnuts
- Dumplings
- Flour
- Flour Tortillas
- Fried Vegetables
- Graham
- Crackers
- Hamburger Buns
- Hotdog Buns
- Ice Cream Cones
- Macaroni
- Melba Toast
- Crackers
- Croutons
- Muffins
- Noodles
- Pancakes
- Pasta
- Pastries
- Pie Crusts
- Pizza Crust
- Pretzels
- Rolls
- Spaghetti
- Stuffing
- Tabbouleh

These are foods that usually and often contain gluten. In some cases, wheat is added as a thickener; barley malt is often added as a form of natural flavor. You must read the labels of these items carefully to look for gluten-containing ingredients. Even better, look for products specifically labeled "gluten-free."

- Beverage Mixes
- Bologna
- Candy (many candies are gluten-free, but READ THE LABEL)
- Canned Baked Beans
- Cold Cuts
- Packaged Cereals (even Corn Cereals)
- Commercially Prepared Broth
- Commercially Prepared Chocolate Milk
- Commercially
- Prepared Soup
- Vegetables with Commercially Prepared Sauces
- Fruit Fillings
- Gravy
- Gum
- Hot Dogs
- Ice Cream
- Non-dairy Creamer
- Potato Chips
- Pudding
- Root Beer
- Syrups
- Salad Dressing
- Soy Sauce
- Custard

Now You Can Be Happy & Gluten-Free Online!

- Order gluten-free apparel in our Gluten-Free Shop
- Recipes
- Updated lists of foods that contain gluten
- Gluten-free deli games
- Picture quiz game
- Browse through restaurants that have gluten-free items on their menu
- Restaurant for the month
- and more!

I'm Happy Being GLUTEN free

home

List Of Foods That Contain Gluten

mm good

ral

My name is Sierra Me[...] been gluten-free for fou[...] hard to find foods that t[...] eat.

No matter what I'm abo[...] look for the words "Glute[...] wheat-free but be careful[...] oats. It's also a good ha[...] I stay clear of any produc[...]

www.imhappybeingglutenfree.com

WRITE YOUR VERY OWN

Recipe Name: _____

Ingredients:

Directions:

Recipe Name: _____

Ingredients:

Directions:

GLUTEN-FREE RECIPES...

Recipe Name: _____

Ingredients:

Directions:

Recipe Name: _____

Ingredients:

Directions:

Made in the USA
San Bernardino, CA
16 December 2019